Teaching the bow to bend ...

MAKING A LONGBOW

Linda Schilling
& Michael Wlotzka

4880 Lower Valley Road • Atglen, PA 19310

Disclaimer: While every effort has been made to present the information contained in this book in accordance with recognized health and safety guidelines, the authors nor the publishers take responsibility for any injuries that may be caused while following the information contained herein.

The reader is advised that professional advice should be sought before embarking on, or copying, any techniques or demonstrations (real or implied) contained in this book.

The reader is reminded that due care and diligence must be adhered to at all times and that current health and safety laws should, at all times, be observed.

This book is sold for informational purposes only.

Copyright © 2014 Kunst-Griff
Linda Schilling + Michael Wlotzka
Originally published in 2010
by Kunst-Griff under same title.

Library of Congress Control Number: 2014932042

Type set in Georgia & Arial

ISBN: 978-0-7643-4595-1
Printed in China

Published by Schiffer Publishing, Ltd.
4880 Lower Valley Road
Atglen, PA 19310
Phone: (610) 593-1777; Fax: (610) 593-2002
E-mail: Info@schifferbooks.com

For our complete selection of fine books on this and related subjects, please visit our website at www.schifferbooks.com. You may also write for a free catalog.

This book may be purchased from the publisher. Please try your bookstore first.

We are always looking for people to write books on new and related subjects. If you have an idea for a book, please contact us at proposals@schifferbooks.com

Schiffer Publishing's titles are available at special discounts for bulk purchases for sales promotions or premiums. Special editions, including personalized covers, corporate imprints, and excerpts can be created in large quantities for special needs. For more information, contact the publisher.

ACKNOWLEDGMENTS

Many Thanks To ...
Liam MacGabhann from Dublin, Ireland;
Ian Coote from Castleford, England;
Sonja Fabig from Braunschweig, Germany;
and Michael Maas from Berlin, Germany ...
For their helpful input and very kind assistance in proof-reading.

CONTENTS

PREFACE

This book is dedicated to all the people who attended one of our bow making workshops, since they motivated us to start writing this book with comments such as, "It would be nice to have this written down for remembering later ..." For most of them, it was their first self-made bow. However, once you are "hooked," you will want to continue under any circumstances.

Soon after, we went to work and described our bow-making workshop. Our goal was to reach the beginners in bow-making, but we also hope that the experienced bow-maker will enjoy reading this book.

With increased experience, the feeling evolves for the right tiller, for the character of the individual piece of wood in hand, and how much and where wood has to be removed... The single steps shown here will then start to flow into each other as you develop a touch for the wood.

PLEASE NOTE:

- Wood is a natural material. Every piece of wood reacts individually and can break despite careful wood selection and cautious treatment.
- Wood dust can cause allergies.
- The tools shown here have to be used with the necessary attention to health and safety precautions, otherwise there is a risk of injury. *Please...always take appropriate measures to ensure health and safety precautions are adhered to!*
- Any use of the information presented in this book is at your own risk and responsibility.
- The results of the conversion from international to U.S. metrics are rounded approximate values.

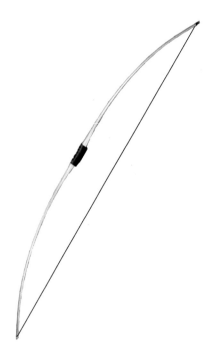

OVERVIEW

	Chapter Content	Material & Tools
	1 ... Wood Selection Wood Types Grain Orientation Flaws in the Wood	Wood
	2 ... The Bow Stave Overview of Bow Profiles Marking the Bow Profile Example: Longbow Preparation Bow Stave	Triangle, ruler Pencil Saw Rasp
	3 ... Tillering Positioning the Stave on the Tillering Stick Finding the "Hinges" Wood Removal and Tool Handling Leveling the Hinges Balancing the Limbs Carving the Nock Grooves Bracing with Tillering String Checking of String Alignment Adjustment of Twisting Tillering to Intended Draw Length Test Shooting Bow Finishing	Triangle, ruler, pencil, adhesive tape, folding yard/meter stick, tiller tool Saw, rasps, files, sandpaper (tillering plane, draw knife) **See appendix:** tillering stick, bow stringer, tillering string, bow string
	4 ... Leather Grip Shaping the Leather Grip	Leather, leather lace, clamps, punch forceps, knife, cling wrap

Chapter 1
WOOD SELECTION

Making a wooden bow basically means to teach a piece of wood to bend up to the intended draw length without breaking. On the one hand, this requires an appropriate tillering process; on the other hand, the right selection of wood plays an important role.

We have to assess the characteristics and the applicability of the wood for building a bow. It can happen that a piece of wood is not suitable for a certain bending and, therefore, can only be used to build a bow with a small draw length and a low draw weight. However, another piece of wood promises to withstand the steady strain for intended draw length and draw weight, and a good and durable bow can be made. Keep in mind, though, that every piece of wood can break if you "overstretch the bow."

Wood Types

What type of wood would be applicable for bow making? The answers to this question already fill volumes of books and there are quite a lot of diverging opinions on that.

Quite often variations in quality are substantially larger within one type of wood than among different types of wood. For selfbows, bows made of one single piece of wood, we have had good experience with ash tree, maple/sycamore, and hickory.

Grain Orientation

With each pulling, an efficient bow is pushed to the limits of its capacity. The back of the bow is placed under tension while the belly of the bow is primarily under compression.

One characteristic of wood is its elasticity. When stressing wood up to a certain threshold, it starts to deform and then, after removal of the stress, it returns, nearly, to its original shape. Beyond the elastic limit, wood does not break immediately, but takes on a permanent deformation. Excessive amounts of stress will lead to breakage of the bow. Flaws and knots in the wood reduce the elasticity.

Wood reacts fine to tension stress; however, only parallel to the grain orientation. Flaws in the fiber course or knots reduce the tensile strength. The compressive strength of wood is not as good as the tensile strength.

In this context, another characteristic of wood is important: the splitting tensile strength. The tissue of wood consists of fiber bundles that can easily be broken up by splitting along the grain.

Teaching the Bow to Bend . . . Making a Longbow

Let's simply imagine a straw bundle as wood fibers clinging against each other. The straw bundle withstands the tension forces, but under compression the single straws tend to snap. The single straws can easily be split off the bundle. The chopping of wood is an obvious example for this splitting effect when, with one stroke parallel to the grain orientation, the piece of wood cracks lengthwise into two pieces.

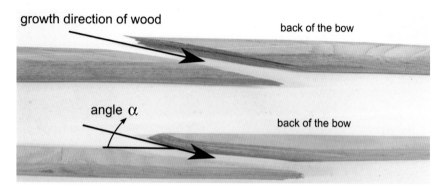

For the broken hickory bows shown above, no attention was paid to the fiber course. The fibers do not run along the longitudinal axis of the bow, but intersect the back of the bow at a slight angle. As a result of the bending, the wood fibers have been pulled apart so much that they could not remain bound together any longer — irrespective of the type of wood, the bow broke.

For reasons of tensile strength and to avoid this "splitting effect," the growth direction of the fibers should run parallel to the longitudinal axis of the bow.

The safest method is to expose a single continuous growth ring for the back of the bow. As seen from the side, the growth rings are lying horizontally in the bow and all grains are running in longitudinal direction of the bow.

Bow with continuous growth ring at the back.

During exposure, it is important to leave the outer growth ring perfectly intact. Once the surface of the growth ring is harmed, tensile and splitting strength decreases at the injured spot.

If there is no wood available that allows the exposure of a growth ring (flat-ringed), it is also possible to make a bow out of a square board or plank, where the growth rings rest vertically (edge-ringed) or diagonally (bias-ringed) to the back of the bow. However, the grains on the back need to run straight and as parallel as possible along the entire length of the bow.

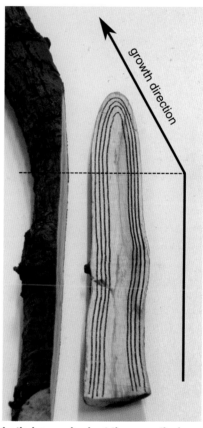

Let's have a look at the growth rings in a piece of wood that has been sawn along the growth direction of the wood: In the relatively straight section of the wood, the growth rings run as almost straight parallel lines.

Teaching the Bow to Bend . . . Making a Longbow

Not following the natural warp of the wood or not sawing along the growth direction will lead to a grain orientation that is no longer relatively straight and parallel, but the growth rings become curvy until they merge into closed rings.

In these sections, the grain orientation would be diagonal to the back of the bow (like with the broken hickory bows). The grains would transversely intersect the surface and not run parallel to the longitudinal axis of the bow. Already at slight bending, the bow stave would likely break because of the splitting effect in these sections.

When selecting a wooden plank or board, ensure that the plank is sawn along the growth direction of the tree. The growth rings should run — as far as possible — in straight and parallel lines along the board. Ensure that the structure of the wood is not impaired by waves, knots, or intersecting growth rings.

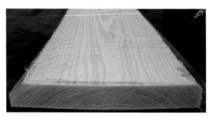

From this plank of ash tree, the outer side parts are applicable for bow-making. Here, the growth rings run straight along the plank. In the core, especially in the rear, the growth rings intersect the surface of the wood.

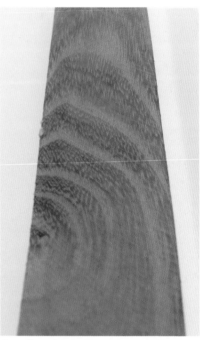

A grain orientation such as the one depicted here is not suitable for making a bow.

On the piece of ash tree illustrated above, the growth rings run linearly over a large part of the stave. This stave is applicable for making a bow.

With this stave of ash tree, the growth rings run relatively straight and parallel over the total length of the back of the bow. Also in the cross section, the diagonal growth rings show a regular structure. From this piece of wood a nice bow can be made.

Flaws in the Wood

During wood selection, pay special attention to any knots, flaws, or irregularities in the wood that would lead to a reduced tensile strength.

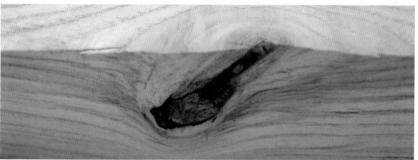

Any knots in the wood will cause the grain structure to be wavy and irregular.

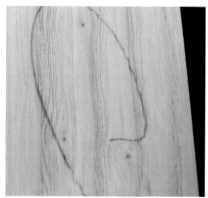

With "edge-ringed" and "bias-ringed" growth rings in the cross section of the stave — at all costs — avoid even small insignificant knots.

Waves and irregularities in the grain orientation imply a potential risk of breakage.

Chapter 2
THE BOW STAVE

With the hints for selecting the wood provided in the previous chapter, we can now start to mark the bow profile on the wooden stave.

Overview: Bow Profiles
Top View (schematic outline)

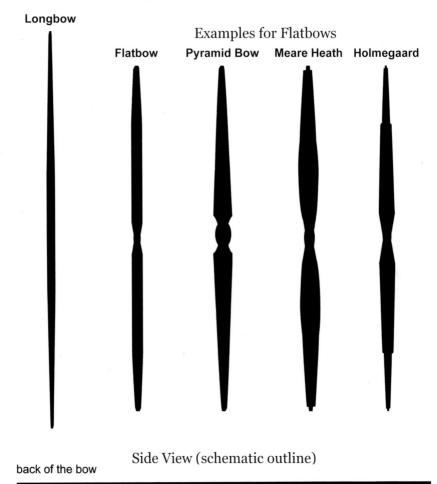

Longbow

Examples for Flatbows

Flatbow   Pyramid Bow   Meare Heath   Holmegaard

Side View (schematic outline)

back of the bow

belly of the bow

handle area

The profile of the top view gives the bow its characteristics. There are hardly any changes to the chosen top view during the bow making process.

The profile of the side view has to be adjusted during the tillering process. In principle, the side view is the same for all bow shapes with the biggest diameter in the handle area and then declining linearly up to the ends of the bow. The dimensions depend on the intended draw weight, the density of the wood, the length of the bow, and the chosen top view. The final side view of the finished bow is worked out during the bow making process.

Marking the Bow Profile on the Wooden Stave

The planks — chosen in accordance with the fiber course of the wood (at least 6-1/2 feet/2 meters long...the longer, the better) — are sawn into square staves.

Examine all four sides of the square stave for:
• Knots in the wood • Fiber course • Seasoning checks • Ingrown bark

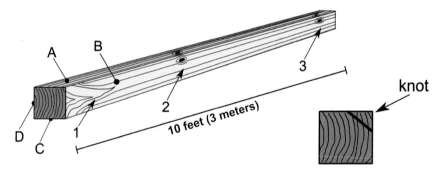

Mark all the conspicuous spots with a pencil (compare the chapter on wood flaws and fiber course). After thorough examination, the following conspicuous spots on our stave have been marked: **Side A/B 1:** very irregular fiber course **2:** small knot **3:** bigger knot, strong impact on fiber course. **Side C/D 4:** very irregular fiber course

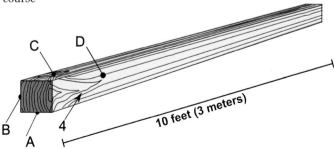

All these spots — 1 to 4 — mean an increased risk for breakage!

Now we have to position our bow profile (top and side view) on the stave in such a way that these four conspicuous spots will be sawn off and, thus, disappear or that they fall into non-bending sections. Simply put, only where there is a bending there may be a breakage.

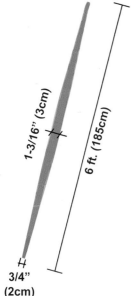

Example: Longbow

We have decided upon a longbow profile and aim at a length of about 6 feet (1.80m) and a draw weight of 50 lbs. at a draw length of 28 inches.

The dimensions of the side view very much depend on the density of the piece of wood. With a more dense wood, the dimensions can usually be somewhat smaller; correspondingly, with less dense wood, they have to be larger to achieve the intended draw weight.

For this example bow, medium-density ash wood is being used, so we assign about 1-3/16" (3cm) for both the height and the width (handle). Towards the tips, we taper the stave to about 3/4" (2cm) in width (top view) and 1/2" (1.2cm) in height (side view).

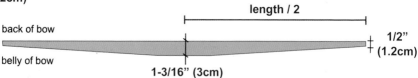

For these dimensions, we take the following points into account:

• The stave should be longer than the intended total length, so that there is some leeway during the tillering process to shorten one or both limbs for balancing reasons or to increase the draw weight, if necessary.

The length primarily depends on the intended draw length of the bow: *(draw length in inches / 0.16) + 2" (5cm) = approx. minimum length of stave.*

During the bow making process, it will then become obvious whether and to what extent the chosen piece of wood can put up with shortening or further tapering.

• The tips are sawn out broader than intended, so that it is possible to adjust the position of the nock in case any correction of the string alignment over the middle of the handle is necessary.

We have identified and marked the conspicuous spots on the stave and decided on a bow shape. For easier handling, we have cut a stencil from plywood with the dimensions of the top view. Now, we outline the bow profile on the stave in such a way that, preferably, all marked weak spots will be cut off.

In out example, the stave looks like this:

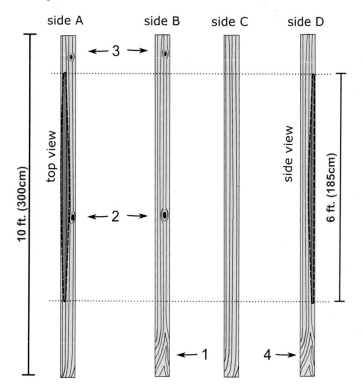

Here, the advantage of a long and broad stave becomes apparent: the bow profile (top view) could be positioned on side A in such a way that spots 1 and 4, as well as spot 3, will disappear after sawing off the ends of the stave. Also, spot 2 (small knot) lies outside of the bow profile in the top view. At the same time, the side profile fits on side D so that there are no conspicuous spots in this section.

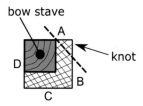

bow stave

knot

We have now eliminated from the stave the marked spots that involve an increased risk of breakage when bending the stave.

Attention: If it is not possible to position the bow profile on the stave in such a way that all conspicuous spots are eliminated, check if the bow profile can be positioned so that:
• All larger conspicuous spots can be eliminated.
• Smaller conspicuous spots fall into sections that do not have to bend later (handle, tips). For these sections, there is not as high a risk of breakage.
  If this is also not possible, then the risk of breakage is altogether too high and, by all means, another piece of wood should be used!

When sawing out, it sometimes happens that the stave starts warping because of the released internal stress within the wood. Taking the conspicuous spots into account, if possible put the top view of the bow profile on the "straight" side and the side profile on the "warped" side.

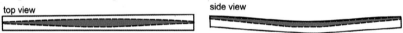

top view   side view

Preparation of the Bow Stave

For our example bow (longbow: length 6 ft. (180cm), 50 lbs. at 28 inches), our sawn out stave looks more or less like this:

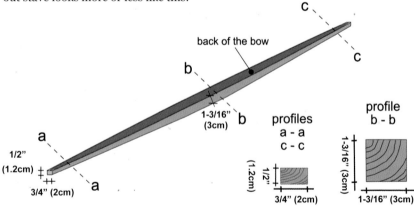

We will work on the back of the bow first. When bending a bow, the back of the bow absorbs the tension forces; therefore, a smooth, level surface is important. Any damage, knocks, or cuts caused by the work tools or any notches will weaken the tension-strained profile and, therefore, increase the risk of breakage.

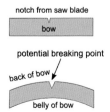

notch from saw blade

bow

potential breaking point

back of bow

belly of bow

Next, smooth down all uneven sections and all tool or sawing remains on the back of the bow using a plane, file, or belt sander. After that, sand the back of the bow with sanding paper of grit sizes 100, 300, and 500, and then polish it with a simple sheet of paper until it shines.

Since we do not work on the back of the bow during the tillering process, it is now already pretty much finished. Therefore, we need to take care that we do not damage the back of the bow during the tillering due to carelessness.

In preparation for tillering, flatten the edges on the belly of the bow and prepare facets on both sides so that the cross section looks like this:

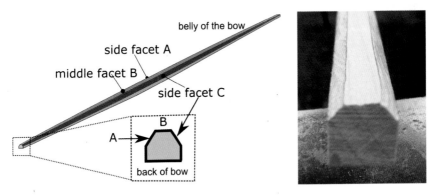

Thus, the belly of the bow is practically divided into three sections:

Middle Facet B: This section is our main work surface. In the tillering process we deliberately remove wood from this section in order to achieve an even bending.

Side Facets A and C: From these sections wood is removed, for example, in order to balance the limbs. If one of the limbs is stronger than the other, the stronger limb is weakened by wood removal from the side facets.

Side Facets A or C: If one limb twists in one direction, wood is removed from one of the side facets. The wood is deliberately removed from the side, to which the limb is supposed to turn.

Now that the stave is sawn out according to the dimensions, the back of the bow is smoothed and polished, and the facets on the belly of the bow are prepared, let's go to the tillering stick and, for the first time, make our bow stave bend.

Chapter 3
TILLERING

Tillering is the process — so to speak — in which we teach the bow stave to bend. This means that we want to achieve that the bow limbs are bending evenly. Therefore, we have to find the sections on the limb that are weaker than the others and for that reason are already bending more than the rest of the limb. In order to relieve these "hinges" and adjust the bending, we have to deliberately remove wood from middle facet B to the left and to the right of these hinges.

Positioning the Stave On the Tillering Stick

To brace the bow stave on the tillering stick, we will be using a so-called bow stringer. The bow stringer has leather caps on both ends that can be easily pulled over the bow tips (to make a bow stringer see Appendix, page 48).

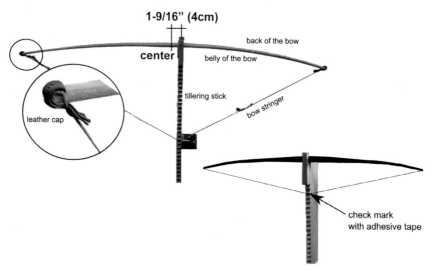

When shooting, the hand grips the handle of our longbow. The arrow rests on the "bow hand" and is shot over the hand. The bow is held centrally in the hand, but is not braced centrally. The arrow lies above the center of the bow. When positioning the bow stave at the tiller stick, we allow for this by placing the center of the bow at a distance of approximately 1-9/16" (4cm) from the tillering stick.

After we have correspondingly positioned the bow stave, we cautiously pull the bow stringer a few notches downwards, clamp it in a notch of the tillering stick, and using a piece of adhesive tape, mark the position of the bow stringer at the tillering stick. In the process of tillering, the adhesive tape is then moving downwards notch per notch.

Take a few steps back and look at the "bow" to get a first impression. For now, there is not much of a "bend" to see.

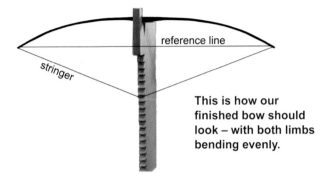

reference line

stringer

This is how our finished bow should look – with both limbs bending evenly.

Finding the "Hinges"

Looking at the stave, we notice that there is one section along each limb that is bending more than the rest. In other words, one section of the limb has a bigger bending radius and that is where a "hinge" appears.

This has to do with the fact that wood, as a natural material, naturally is never homogenous. Due to differences in density, the piece of wood is bending more in some sections than in others. Unfortunately, it is also quite difficult to saw out the bow stave so accurately that its shape already evenly meets the side profile. Usually, in some sections, the profile turns out to be somewhat thicker than in others.

Since the bow stave has not yet been tillered, it is not so easy to clearly distinguish the hinges. If we simply drew the bow stave up to 28 inches, the small hinges would become big hinges or the bow stave would very likely break at these sections.

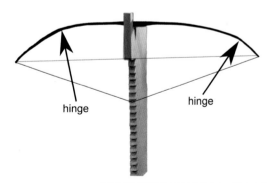

hinge

hinge

It is our goal to find these hinges as long as they are still "small" and keep removing them, until the bow bends evenly.

We place the bow stave on the tillering stick and it is put under slight bending stress by the bow stringer. Now, we start to search for the biggest hinge on each limb — these are the potential danger spots for the bow.

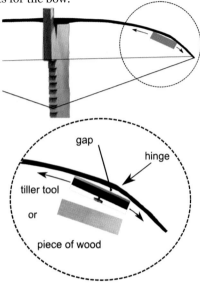

To do this, we use our tiller tool. The built-in lead of the tiller tool marks the sections we are looking for (compare to page 78). However, a straight piece of wood about 6" long (15cm) and a pencil will also serve the purpose.

Place the tiller tool on the belly of the bow and move it along the left limb from the tip to the handle. In doing so, it immediately becomes obvious that the gaps between the tiller tool and the belly of the bow vary in size. Repeat this procedure for the right limb. Here, too, we find gaps of different sizes.

For the bow stave, we find the following situation:

Left Limb

At position (a), there is a small gap; here, the bow stave is already bending a little. At position (c), there is practically no gap at all, meaning practically no bending. At position (b), the biggest gap is shown; here, the stave is bending most, so here is our hinge.

Right Limb

At positions (1) and (2), there are almost no gaps — the bending is still small. At position (3), there is the biggest gap; here, the stave is bending most, so here is our hinge.

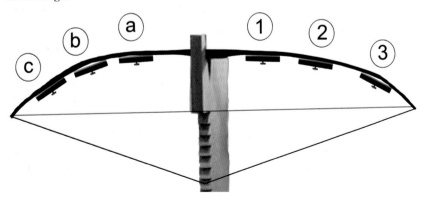

Place the tiller tool on the biggest gap of the left limb (hinge b) and adjust the pencil lead in such a way that it is almost touching the belly of the bow, but not quite. If we now slide the tiller tool with long movements along the limb, the lead is marking not the hinge, but automatically the stiffer sections. We repeat this marking process a couple of times and notice that in some sections the tiller tool is leaving more lead markings than in others. Since the lead is wearing off and becomes shorter, it more often touches the sections that are bending less than the sections that are bending more. This helps in estimating the amount of wood to be removed: If the markings are bolder, then this section is stiffer and bending less than the rest, so a little bit more wood can be removed. If the markings are weaker, this section is already bending a little more, so we carefully remove only a bit of wood.

Now repeat this procedure for the biggest gap on the right limb (hinge 3).

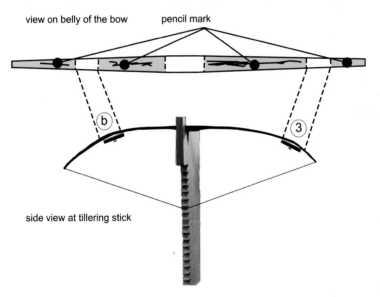

Through the pencil marks, we can see in which sections wood has to be removed. In the section of the hinge, we do not remove wood, otherwise the bow stave would be further weakened in this section. We do not want to extend the hinge further, but get the bow stave to bend evenly in all sections along the limbs.

Here, of course, arises the question: How much wood do we have to remove to achieve an even bending of the bow limbs? Good question and, if the answer to that was known, the bow would be finished in one go. With growing experience, the bowyer gets more and more a feeling for how much wood has to be removed.

To begin with, we make the following consideration: Generally, we have to remove more wood at the tips of the bow than in the handle area to achieve the same change in the bending. Why?

When pulling the bow string, the limb practically reacts like a lever. At the tips of the bow, the bending stress is lowest and then it is increasing up to the center of the bow, where the highest bending stress occurs.

For the bow stave, this means: the more the bending stress decreases, the more wood has to be removed to achieve the same effect. In other words, in the handle area, take off only a very small amount of wood; from the limbs, remove a little bit more; and from the tips, somewhat more to achieve a similar change in the bending.

This factor is also important for how we handle our tools.

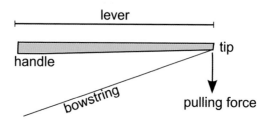

Removal of Wood

For now, the main work surface is middle facet B. Only there do we remove wood and, of course, only in the marked sections. From the hinge sections and in the handle area, we do not take off any wood for the moment.

Schematically, the relative removal of wood over the total bow length could be illustrated like this:

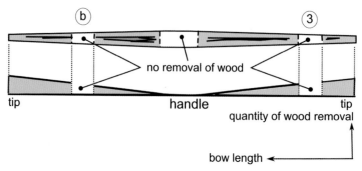

The amount of wood removed depends on the bending radius of the bow stave and on the tools applied. As a broad rule, one could say: As long as the bending is still small, work with tools that allow the removal of bigger amounts of wood (i.e., coarse hoof rasp, coarse rasp, or drawknife). With these tools, we work cautiously and take care to make only a few movements per work step. Relative to the increase in bending, change to tools that remove less amounts of wood (i.e., spokeshave, scraper, medium to fine file, or sandpaper).

The closer the bow stave gets to the intended draw length, the less wood we will need to remove. This is because, as the bending increases, the forces in the wood become increasingly larger.

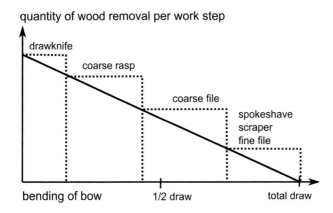

Needless to say, the amount of wood that effectively has to be removed cannot be quantified by a unit of measurement. This means: experimenting and developing a feel for it...

Tool Handling

In longer sections where wood has to be removed, draw the rasp in overlapping movements over the bow limb. Begin at the starting point and make the first stroke up to point E-1. Now, go back to the starting point and make another long and smooth forward stroke up to E-2, so that it runs for the second time over the length (S-1).

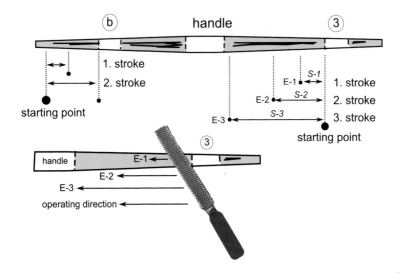

The same for E-3: Go back to the starting point and make a long and smooth forward stroke up to E-3. Now, we have run three times over the length S-1 and twice over the length S-2, meaning that up to the tips of the bow we have removed more wood and in the handle area (E-2 to E-3) only a bit.

This method is not practicable on shorter sections, so in those areas work carefully and make sure to remove less wood in the handle area than at the tips.

Leveling the Hinges

After identifying the sections where wood has to be removed, clamp the bow stave into the bench vice.

The stiffer sections are now marked with pencil lines. These are the sections from which we want to take off wood. When working on these sections, we will also, inevitably, remove the pencil lines. In order to still distinguish the sections where by no means we want to remove wood, highlight them with vertical pencil lines across the limbs (see illustration on page 30). We always keep an eye on how far we can move our tool.

From the unmarked sections, like hinge (3) and (b), as well as in the handle area, do not remove wood for now. In the marked sections, rasp off a good deal of wood in the areas around the hinges (distinct pencil marks = stiffer sections). From the sections with weaker markings, remove less wood.

By removing wood, the sections next to the hinges are weakened in order to equalize the bending in this area. As soon as the sections next to the hinge are bending as much as the hinge itself, we have come already somewhat closer to our goal and eliminated one potential breaking point.

Now, take a closer look at the result of the first tillering step. Put on the caps of the bow stringer again and position the bow stave on the tillering stick as described.

The adhesive check mark shows where the bow stringer was hooked up before. After each tillering step, the bow stave has to be stressed a bit more — bent a bit more — so that the impact of the wood removal takes effect. Pull the bow stringer one or two notches below the current check mark, hook it up, and relocate the adhesive tape.

> **Important:** With each tillering step, the bow stringer has to be pulled one or two notches further down — step by step — up to the intended draw length. Only this additional stress, through the greater bending, brings about the desired effect on the bow stave from the preceding removal of wood and, consequently, a change in the tiller.

Again, position the tiller tool on the belly of the bow. Look for the biggest hinge on each bow limb and mark the stiffer, more flat sections.

After we have enlarged the bending radius of the stave and marked the hinges again, the result looks like this:

Left Limb

The "old" hinge (b) has more or less vanished. Here, enough wood has been taken off, so the bending has adapted. In section (c), a "new" hinge has appeared. Here, too much wood has been removed.

Right Limb

The "old" hinge (3) is still there. While it has become a little bit smaller, it has not yet been totally balanced. Correspondingly, this section broadens and forms the "new" hinge (4).

Now back to the bench vice: highlighting the section borders with vertical pencil lines and starting to remove wood from the freshly marked sections.

At the moment, we are still only working on middle facet B of the stave. When removing wood, take care and avoid creating any bumps, waves, or terraces along the total length of the stave, especially around the vertical borderlines. Instead, try to achieve a smooth surface. Sometimes it might be better to remove less wood from a stiff section to make sure that the transitions — especially the dips to the handle area — are floating and smooth.

Now back to the tillering stick: Position the stave, pull the tillering string one or two notches downwards, hook them in, and relocate the tape. Afterwards, check the bending again and mark the hinges as described.

Left Limb

Hinge (c) is balanced out. In section (d), a new hinge has appeared. Here, too much wood has been removed.

Right Limb

"Old" hinge (4) has broadened again into hinge (5) with an already relatively even bending, which we now have to extend further over the whole length of the limb.

Repeat this tillering process again and again: we pull step-by-step one or two notches further down, until we have reached about the fifteenth notch of the tillering stick. This corresponds to a draw length of about 20-7/8" (53cm); the bow is now one-third finished. The big hinges are gone and the bending looks already quite even.

Now, it is time to check the balance between the left and the right limb:

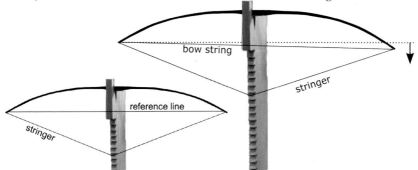

Compared with the picture of the finished bow, it seems like (on our bow) the right limb is hanging down more than the left one. We can check this by attaching a string from tip to tip. Before the hinges were removed, the left limb seemed to be weaker (see page 23). Now the right limb is weaker — it has a larger bending and hangs underneath the reference line — so it's time to give thought to the balancing of the limbs.

Each limb taken by itself already shows a quite even bending, but the goal is to achieve that both limbs are in balance and have a similar bending. This way the limbs are of more or less the same strength and the tips are on the same level.

Like with bow shapes where the limbs considerably differ in length or bending (e.g. Japanese or some Indian bows), with an unbalanced bow the pressure point while drawing is not located in the center of the bow. Since the handle of the longbow is in the center of the bow, we want the pressure point also to be there, so that at full draw we feel the bow handle being pressed against the palm of our bow hand. Both limbs should be of approximately the same stiffness and the bow should look just about symmetrical.

Balancing the Limbs

We have different possibilities to achieve a balance between the stronger and the weaker limb:
• The stronger limb is weakened by removing wood on both side facets A and C.
• The weaker limb is strengthened by making it slightly shorter.
• A combination of the two possibilities.

Teaching the Bow to Bend . . . Making a Longbow

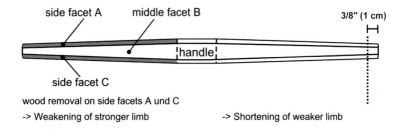

side facet A — middle facet B — 3/8" (1 cm)

handle

side facet C

wood removal on side facets A und C

-> Weakening of stronger limb   -> Shortening of weaker limb

Weakening the stronger limb by removing wood from side facets A and C can be carried out repeatedly, but the more times wood is taken from the side facets, the more the draw weight decreases.

Shortening the weaker limb by 3/8" or 3/4" (1-2cm) usually does not play such a big role for the symmetry of the bow, but further shortening might have a negative effect on the overall impression of the bow profile. Shortening a limb increases the draw weight and decreases the maximum draw length.

Therefore, we usually recommend combining these methods to balance the limbs.

Since we have sawn out the bow stave about 2" (5cm) longer, there is plenty of leeway for shortening one limb without jeopardizing the intended maximum draw length. We simply cut off 3/8" (1cm) from the weaker limb and, for the stronger limb, smoothly remove wood from side facets A and C over the whole length of the limb, but we do not remove any wood from middle facet B!

Now, we hook up the bow stave one notch further down on the tillering stick and look at the result. After having removed wood from the side facets and shortened one limb, both limbs appear to be almost equally strong and in a more or less satisfactory balance, so it does not seem likely that a larger bending would again lead to any significant imbalance of the limbs.

If the result is not yet satisfactory, continue to find and remove the hinges. After two or three times of doing this, repeat the balancing of the limbs as described. However, as already mentioned, the further along we are in the tillering process and the larger the bending of the bow stave, the bigger the impact of removing any wood. More shortening — up to maximum 2" (5cm) — is theoretically possible, but it is not recommended: What is gone, is gone...

Now, continue to find and remove the hinges, step-by-step, up to about 27-9/16" (70cm), measured from the bow belly to the notch where the tillering string is hooked up in the tillering stick. This corresponds to about two-thirds of the intended draw length, so we will want to brace our bow with a bow string for the first time.

For this, we need a tillering string (see Appendix, pages 50 and 63), though the bow has not yet any nock grooves for attaching the string.

Carving the Nock Grooves

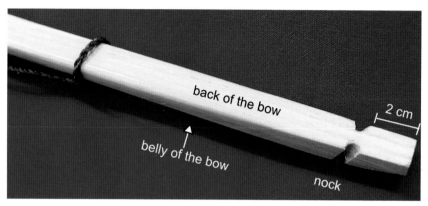

For carving the nock grooves, use a round file (diameter 3/16" or 4mm). Since we will also still need the bow stringer with its leather caps later, the distance from the end of the limb to the nock groove should be about 3/4" long (2cm).

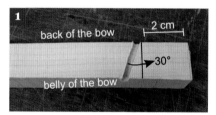

File a groove into one side of the tip — about 3/4" (2cm) from the end of the limb — at a slight angle of approx. 30° and about 3/16" (4mm) deep.

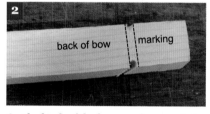

On the back of the bow, make a mark for the second nock groove on the opposite side at the same level as the first one.

Likewise, mark the position for the second nock groove at the same level as the first one, on the belly of the bow.

Clamp in the bow sideways and file in the second nock groove between these two markings, again 3/16" deep (4mm).

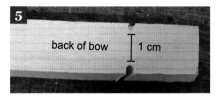

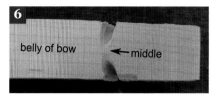

On the back of the bow, make sure that the distance between the nock grooves remains sufficiently large. Move the file in a straight line along the bow side. An "inclined" filing might result in the gap being too small and this could result in breakage of the bow at this point.

On the belly of the bow, carefully round down the nock grooves, in a slightly sloped angle, until the two nock grooves almost meet in the middle — there should remain a strip of wood between them. This is necessary to prevent the string from slipping out of the nock grooves when bracing the bow.

Now repeat these steps for the other limb and the bow is ready to be braced with the tillering string.

Bracing the Bow With the Tillering String

For bracing the bow, use a flemish-splice tillering string as described in the appendix (page 50). Since during the tillering process the current draw weight of the bow exceeds the intended draw weight, the tillering string is about one and a half to twice as thick as the later bow string. At the same time, a thicker tillering string offers more security for tillering the braced bow — especially at the ends of the limbs where the distance between bow and bow string is small, there is a risk of damaging the string with the applied tools. If this should occur, immediately replace a damaged or otherwise flawed string.

Pull the loop of the tillering string — the so-called string eye — about 6" (15cm) beyond the nock groove over one limb. At the end of the other limb, attach the tillering string with a so-called bowyer's knot (see Appendix, page 72).

Now, we must check if the bow already bends enough or if it is necessary to lengthen the tillering string. For this, we put on the caps of the bow stringer again and reposition the bow on the tillering stick. For now, let the tillering string hang loose over the bow on the tillering stick in such a way that it does not get in the way with the bow stringer and does not get caught up in the notches. Pull the bow stringer one notch further down, hook it up in the tillering stick, and relocate the tape.

After having properly positioned the bow, bow stringer, and tillering string, we must check if the tillering string is long enough in respect to the bow, or, more precisely, if the bow is already bending enough, so that we can insert the string eye into the nock without effort. Now, take the tillering string and move the string eye towards the nock without dragging it. The string should slide easily and without strain into the nock.

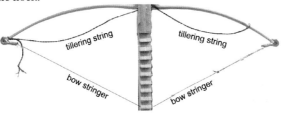

Attention: Dragging or pulling the tillering string involves the risk that the caps of the bow stringer will slip off the braced bow, causing the bow to release violently — and possibly resulting in serious injury to the face or upper body. Sometimes the tillering string can get caught in the tillering stick. If this should occur, carefully release it out of the notch, but please ensure that the bow stringer remains safely fixed in the tillering stick!

In this case, the string eye of the tillering string does not slide into the nock without effort. It is too short or the bow is not yet bending enough.

Put the tillering string back and pull the bow stringer one notch further down on the tillering stick so that the bow bends a little bit more. Now, try again to insert the tillering string. This time it should work.

If this still doesn't lead to success, there are two possibilities:

• Lengthen the tillering string by relocating the knot a little bit.

• Recommended: Put the tillering string aside for now and continue tillering a few notches further, until the bow bends some more.

Now, check again if the string eye can be inserted into the nock without effort.

Teaching the Bow to Bend . . . Making a Longbow

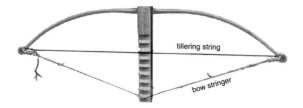

tillering string

bow stringer

When attaching the tillering string, we have pulled the bow stringer two notches further down without checking the tiller.

Now, we want to continue tillering with the tillering string and remove the bow stringer. For this, we have to find the right position respectively notch on the tillering stick for the tillering string, so carefully we pull the tillering string until we feel the strain of the bow stringer relax a bit. This is the notch where we want to hook in the tillering string on the tillering stick and, accordingly, relocate the tape. Now that the bow is braced with the tillering string, we can remove the bow stringer.

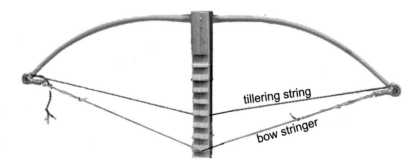

tillering string

bow stringer

You might wonder, why not brace the bow just like this without the tillering stick? By using the tillering stick and the bow stringer for the first bracing of the bow, we avoid the risk of drawing the bow too far beyond the current tillering status, which might result in damage of the bow.

Before attaching the tillering string, the bow should be bending by approximately two-thirds of its full draw. The tillering string is now hooked in at about 20 inches draw length, so for an intended draw length of 28 inches the bow is now already two-thirds finished.

Next, check the bow, now braced with the tillering string, for hinges and mark them as previously described.

Now, it is time to check the string alignment. For this, take the bow off the tillering stick and lay the back of the bow on a plane surface — with the tillering string showing upwards.

Checking the String Alignment

Now step back a little and have a look at the side profile of the bow.

left limb   **right limb**

The left limb is much stronger and stiffer than the right limb; therefore, it is bending less. Our previous corrections have not been sufficient enough to balance the bow.

Now, take a look at the string alignment along the bow. The left limb is not only too stiff, but it is also twisting. The string is off-center and does not run over the middle of the handle.

> **Attention:** The string should track down the middle of the handle. If both limbs are twisting a little bit in opposite directions, but the string runs over the middle of the handle, the twist is not such an issue for the balance of the bow and there is more leeway for correction.

Take the bow and pull it carefully up to a maximum of 20 inches. The bow is slightly rotating in the bow hand and is still much too strong.

This is the result so far:

- The bow has been tillered up to 2/3 of the intended draw length and is now bending enough to be braced with an adequate brace height of 4-3/4" to 6" (12-15cm).
- The left limb is still stronger than the right limb, although we already took countermeasures by shortening the weaker right limb and weakening the stronger left limb through wood removal from side facets A and C.
- The left limb is twisting.
- The string does not run over the middle of the handle.
- When drawn, the bow is rotating around its axis in the bow hand.
- The bow is still far too strong.

For a better assessment, check the string distance. This means that on both limbs, about 7-7/8" (20cm) from the center of the bow, measure the distance between the string and the belly of the bow (compare also brace height).

For the bow in this example, we find the following string distances:

left limb = lower limb 5-5/16"   **right limb = upper limb 5-11/16"**
(135mm)   **(145mm)**
difference 3/8" (10mm)

Since, as explained earlier, the bow is not drawn centrally, but shot over the hand, as far as our experience goes, the bow lies more comfortably in the bow hand if the string distance for the upper limb is about 1/8" to 3/16" (3-5mm) more than for the lower limb. This means, at a tillering status of about two-thirds, we have to weaken the stronger left limb until the difference between the string distances comes to about 1/8" to 3/16" (3-5mm).

At the same time, the stronger left limb is twisting. This can be due to the internal stress and the fiber course of the wood or we have removed too much wood from one side facet — this can happen if the tools are applied in too large an angle when working on the limbs.

Adjustment of the Twisting

For now, we focus on the adjustment of the twisting. In order to counteract the twisting, wood has to be removed from the side of the limb that we want the bow to turn back to. In this case, the limb turns to the right, meaning that side facet C is weaker. Therefore, we have to remove wood from side facet A to bring the limb into balance. In the progressed tillering status, every measure has a big impact, so proceed carefully and remove only small amounts of wood.

Position the bow again one notch further down on the tillering stick and mark the hinges with the tiller tool. For leveling the hinges, we take off wood from the marked sections on middle facet B and then start to carefully remove wood from side facet A along the entire left limb. We do not remove any wood from side facet C or from the side facets of the right limb.

By doing this, we work against the twisting while at the same time the string moves towards the middle of the bow and the stronger left limb is weakened. We repeat this process until the left limb is balanced while paying attention not to weaken the left limb so much that it suddenly becomes weaker than the right one!

Now the twisting is straightened out, the stronger limb is weakened, and the overall draw weight is reduced. Unfortunately, the string does not yet run entirely over the middle of the handle.

For now, we do not want to make any more adjustments on the side facets since the bow looks balanced. Since we had the foresight to leave a little bit of leeway at the nocks and made them broad enough, we still have the possibility of shifting the string a little bit more towards the middle of the handle by deepening one nock groove.

On the side of the limb where the string moves away from the middle, we file the nock groove a little bit deeper.

With our bow, the string pointed to the right. We made the nock groove on the right side a little bit deeper and as a result the string moved further into the middle.

Tillering Up to the Intended Draw Length

We have now straightened out the twisting and the string runs over the middle of the handle. Due to the big impact of wood removal at this stage, the draw weight has been reduced. When rounding down the edges and honing the bow with fine sandpaper, the bow will again lose some of its draw weight.

Next, we have to get up to the intended draw weight and continue to find and remove the hinges on middle facet B until we have achieved a draw length of 26 inches.

Again, we examine the side profile of the bow and measure the string distances. There is only a minimal twisting left. The limbs look even and the string distance of the upper limb is about 1/8" (3mm) larger than the one of the lower limb.

The string runs over the middle of the handle; when drawing we do not feel any significant rotating in the bow hand anymore and are quite happy with the shape of our bow. However, the draw weight is still a little bit too high.

In order to reduce the draw weight, take off a tiny bit of wood from side facets A and C of both limbs. At the same time, round down the edges of the limbs and bring the handle to the desired shape. When working on the side facets, it is recommended to take off the tillering string since it will be easier to work along the sides of the limbs.

The dips to the handle already look quite regular since, during the tillering process, attention was paid to achieving a smooth surface without any bumps or waves. At one go with rounding down the edges, we can now arrive at the intended shape of our handle.

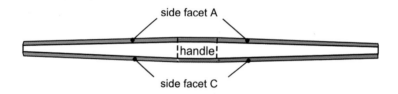

Next, brace the bow again with the tillering string and increase the brace height to about 6-5/16" (16cm). Now, back to the tillering stick: hook in the tillering string one notch further down, look for hinges, and check the draw weight. After that, remove the hinges again — as far as still existing, the hinges have become considerably smaller. If the draw weight is still too high, remove a tiny bit of wood from the side facets of both limbs again and round down the edges until a nice D-shape has been achieved.

Repeat these tillering steps until the intended draw weight is achieved. Now, it is time to do the first test shooting of the bow.

Test Shooting

During the test shooting, we will want to assess how the bow sits in the bow hand. Make several test shots — hold the handle in different positions — to figure out the best arrow rest position. Mark the spot for the arrow rest position on the back of the bow for attaching the leather grip.

After test shooting, check the tiller again. If necessary, slight corrections can still be carried out.

Bow Finishing

We can now put the finishing touches to the bow. Start with sandpaper of grit size 120 and grind out the coarse traces with long movements along the length of the bow. Continue with grit size 240 and finally with grit size 500.

The fine sanding dust of grit size 500 will gather in any remaining tool traces, making them well visible. Go over these visible traces again, one by one, with grit size 120, 240, and 500 until the surface is smooth and no tool traces remain. With a simple white sheet of paper, polish the surface until it shines.

Finally, the bow gets a protective coating with wax or a wax mixture. It is recommended to use a wax compliant to EN 71, meaning it is suitable for toys. Apply the wax with a small brush — any possible wax lumps should be brushed away with a paintbrush —and polish the bow with a cotton cloth.

Finally, the bow gets a leather grip and a bow string (see Appendix, page 63).

The bow is finished: 50 lbs. at 28 inches, length 6 feet (180cm).

Chapter 4
LEATHER GRIP

For the leather grip, cut out a piece of leather large enough to fit around the handle and protruding a couple of inches/centimeters on each side. Soak the leather in water for a few minutes, so it becomes smooth enough to mold the shape.

Before fixing the leather with clamps around the handle, protect the wood of the bow with cling wrap.

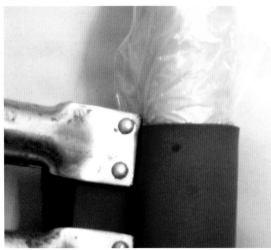

Since the handle lacing is on the back of the bow, put the piece of leather around the handle in such a way that you can attach the clamps on the back of the bow to shape the handle. This should allow you to see, through the emerging folds in the leather, the fringe where you will cut the leather.

When drying off, the leather will shrink, depending on the type of leather used, so remember this when punching in the holes for the lacing. Make sure the space between the holes and the edge of the leather fringe is at least 5/16" (8mm). To ensure the same intervals between holes, use dividers to mark little "guide points" in the leather.

Put the leather piece around the handle in position — against the spot you had marked during the test shooting for the arrow rest position. Pull a leather lace in crosswise direction through the holes and fasten it with a knot at the end. To avoid any pressure marks on the leather, allow it to dry off for a little while.

APPENDIX

	Tools	Page 45
	Tillering Stick	Page 47
	Making a Bow Stringer	Page 48
	Tillering String Bow String	Page 50 Page 63
	Bowyer's Knot	Page 73
	Glossary	Page 74

Tools

There are various tools used for bow making. Hand tools are recommended because they are easy to handle without producing too much noise and dust. Some hand tools do not require sharpening and are ideal for bow making (see picture below). Working with a draw knife or a plane is very comfortable and effective, but with these tools it is fundamental that the blade is always kept very sharp; therefore, they must be resharpened frequently.

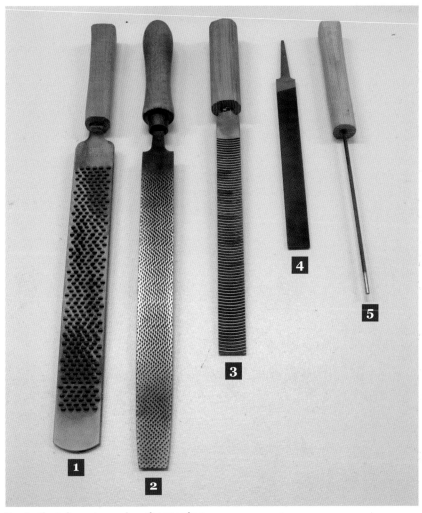

Tools that do not require sharpening.

Teaching the Bow to Bend . . . Making a Longbow

1 Hoof Rasp: Very coarse rasp for contouring the bow stave.

2 Medium Course Rasp: For the first tillering steps up to two-thirds of the intended draw length.

3 Milled Radial File: For removing rasp traces and for tillering of the last one-third.

4 Machinist File (cut 0): For removing residual tool traces after the tillering process.

5 Roundfile (3/16" or 4mm): For making the nock grooves.

6 Draw Knife: For contouring the bow stave, removes a lot of wood.

7 Scraper Plane/Spokeshave: From one-third of the intended draw length until completion of the tiller and for removing tool traces; takes off small amounts of wood and leaves an even surface.

8 Scraper: From two-thirds of the intended draw length and for removing tool traces, takes off small amounts of wood.

With these tools, make sure that they are always kept sharpened. Blunt tools involve an increased risk of injury and tear out wood grains.

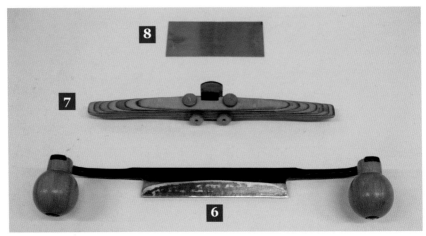

Tools that require sharpening.

Attention: When sharpening these tools always take the necessary health and safety precautions and follow the sharpening instructions of the manufacturer!

Tillering Stick

The tillering stick is a great help for looking at the braced bow stave from a distance in order to check the bending and at the same time to constantly keep an eye on the draw length.

For the tillering stick in this example, take a plywood board, saw out the notches according to the dimensions in the drawings, and provide a support for the bow stave.

For using the bow stringer, additional notches will be needed beyond the intended draw length of 28 inches.

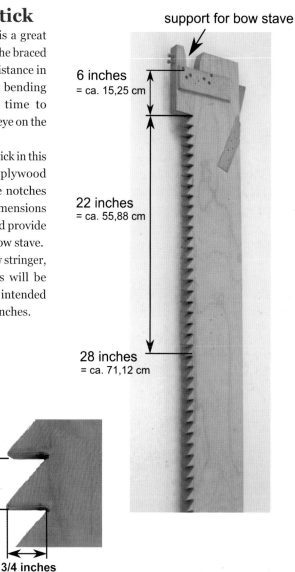

support for bow stave

6 inches
= ca. 15,25 cm

22 inches
= ca. 55,88 cm

28 inches
= ca. 71,12 cm

1 inch
= ca. 2,54 cm

3/4 inches
= ca. 2 cm

Making a Bow Stringer

For the bow stringer, use nylon cord and two leather strips for the caps, about 3/4" (2cm) in width and 5-1/2" (14cm) in length. The bow stringer should be approximately the same length as the bow stave; therefore, the nylon cord measured somewhat longer.

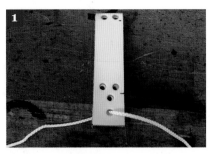

Fold the leather strip in the middle. Close to the fold, punch two holes into the leather; at the open end, punch two holes, one above the other, and another two holes.

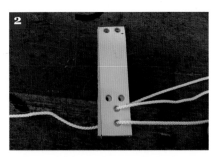

Pull the nylon cord through the bottom hole and then back through the hole above ...

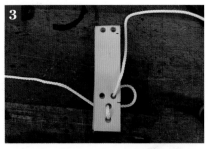

... and then from bottom up through the right hole at the lower end ...

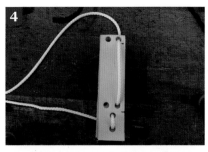

... and through the right hole at the upper end.

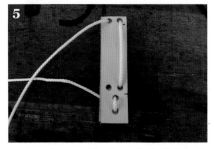

Back to the topside through the left hole of the upper pair ...

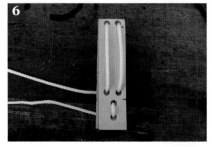

... and over the top side into the left hole at the bottom ...

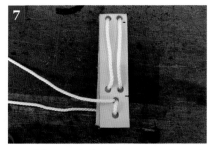

... and then again from bottom up through the upper single hole ...

... and over the top side back through the bottom single hole.

Now tighten the cord, so that the leather strip gets the form of a cap.

The bow tips should fit snugly between the caps.

On the reverse side, fix the cord with a knot.

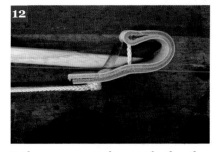

In the same way, make a cap for the other limb at the other end of the cord.

Adjust the length of the bow stringer to the length of the bow. If this does not work, make a few knots in the bow stringer in order to trim it to the correct bow length.

Tillering String (Flemish Splice):

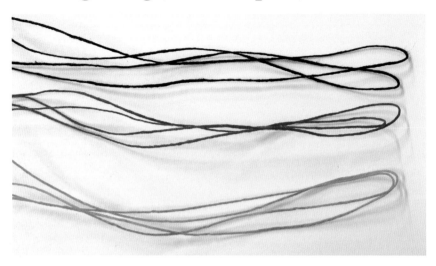

For the tillering string, we use three strands of bowstring — for better illustration, in this example there are three different colors.

The number of threads in one strand depends on the bowstring material used and the draw weight. Please observe the manufacturer's safety information! For better illustration, the photos show only four threads for each strand, but for the example bow (intended draw weight 50 lbs. at 28 inches) the tillering string would be made of 3 x 8 threads.

Bracket the three strands together with a clamp as illustrated in the photo below.

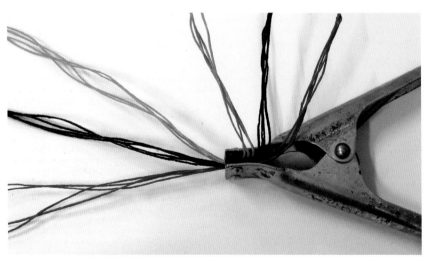

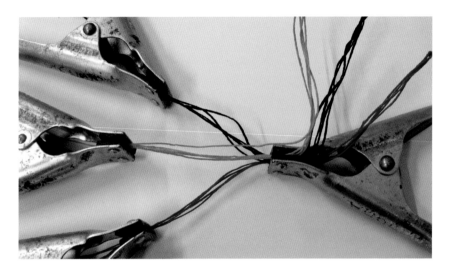

The long ends of each strand are also fixed with clamps at an interval of a few inches from the first clamp.

After that, twist each strand in itself to the right, one after the other, making sure that during twisting the strands remain straight. As soon as they start flexing, turn the twist back until they look straight again.

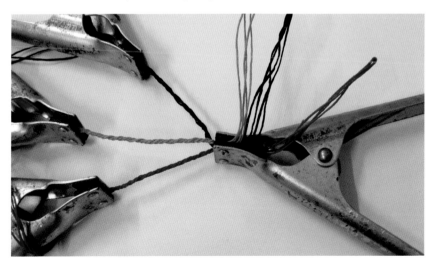

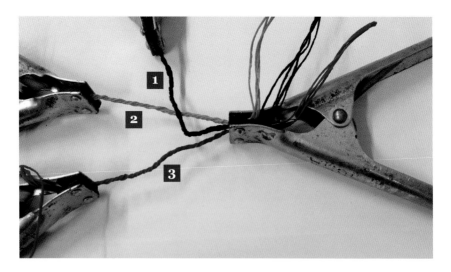

Next, start to twist the strands around each other. Since each strand is twisted in itself to the right (clockwise), now twist to the left (counter-clockwise).

Twist strand 1 around strand 2 by putting strand 1 to the left over strand 2 and then strand 2 to the left over strand 1.

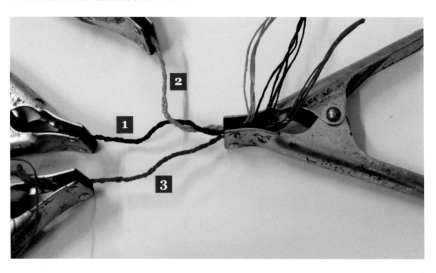

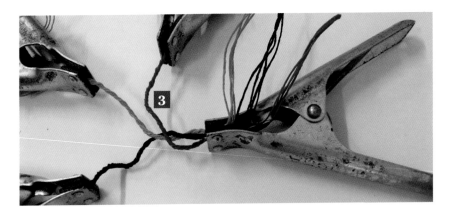

Now that strand 1 and strand 2 are twisted around each other, put strand 3 to the left, over the two strands that are already twisted around each other.

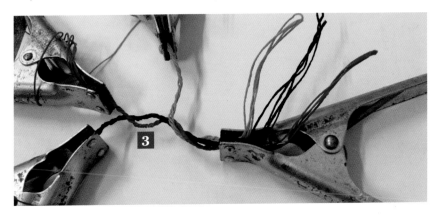

The same for strand 2: Put strand 2 to the left, around the two other strands.

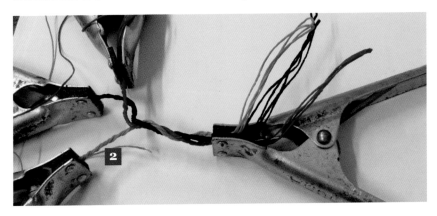

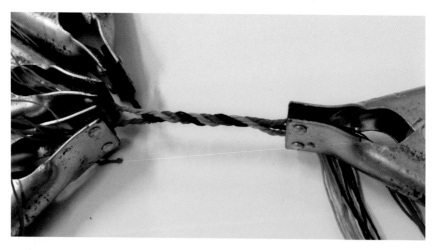

Go on with strand 1 and so on and twist the strands around each other to the left, until a length of about 4" (10cm) has been reached.

Now, form a loop (string eye) with the twisted strands, taking the dimensions of the loop from the nocks.

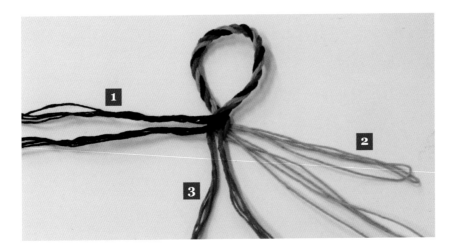

Next, gather together the two strands of the same color. If you use only one color, gather one long and one short strand together to a pair of strands.

Each of these strand pairs will now be twisted in itself to the right.

Again, strands 1, 2, and 3 are twisted around each other to the left (above).
Now twist strand 2 around strand 3 to the left and then put the pair of strands 2-3
over strand 1 (below).

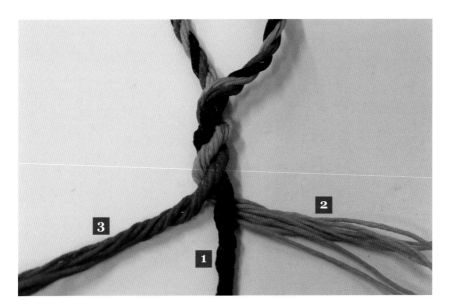

After having done so, take pair 1-2 and twist it to the left, around strand 3 (below).

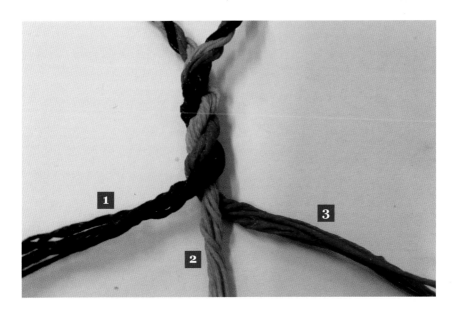

Teaching the Bow to Bend . . . Making a Longbow

During the next rounds, we start to pull out the short strands, one by one, to the side and stop twisting them with the rest of the strands. In this way, the string is tapered step by step.

Pull out the short end of strand 1 to the side and go on twisting the strands by putting strand pair 2-3 over strand 1. At the same time, make sure that each strand remains twisted in itself to the right! Now, pull out the short end of strand 2 to the side.

Now, go on twisting and pulling out the short ends until all the short ends stick out of the string.

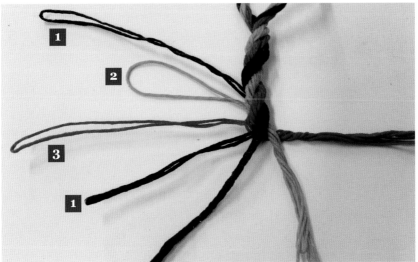

Teaching the Bow to Bend . . . Making a Longbow

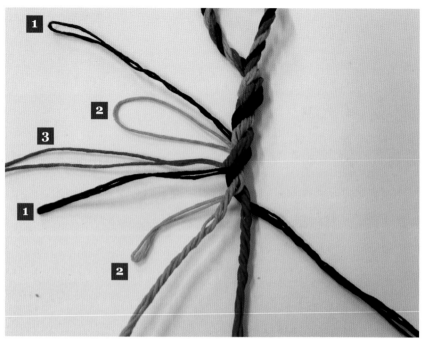

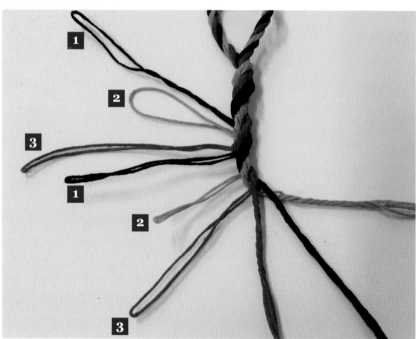

Once all the short ends stick out, carry on twisting strands 1 to 3 until they have reached the intended string length.

Carefully cut off the short ends just before the string, but be careful not to damage the string!

With natural materials, the still overhanging ends retract into the string under strain. With synthetic materials, carefully singe off the ends with a lighter. Make sure not to damage the string. A little bead will form, preventing the threads from slipping out.

Teaching the Bow to Bend . . . Making a Longbow

To prevent the tillering string from untwisting, make a knot at the end and tighten it securely.

Bow String (Flemish Splice)

In principle, a bow string is made in the same way as the tillering string, but here there is only two strands. The number of threads per strand depends on the draw weight. Please observe the manufacturer's information and safety instructions for that! Dacron is being used for the string in this example. According to the manufacturer's information, for 50 lbs, 14 threads in total are needed, so 7 threads per strand.

In the photos, there are again only four threads per strand for a better illustration.

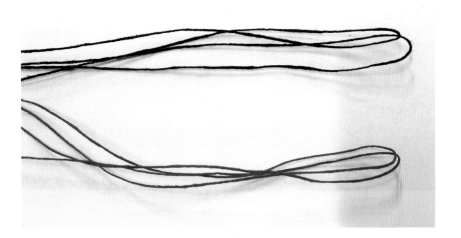

Bracket the strands together with a clamp.

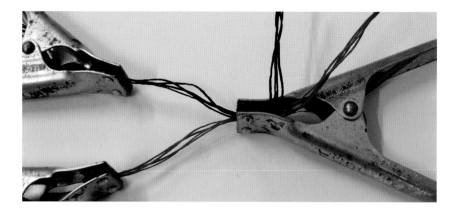

On each loose end, attach a clamp and start twisting each of the two strands in itself to the right.

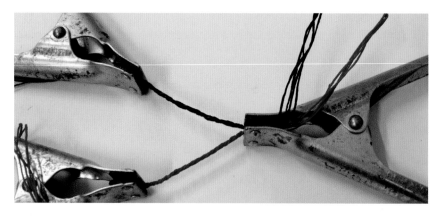

After that, twist the strands around each other to the left by putting the red strand to the left over the black strand.

Next, put the black one to the left over the red one and so on, until you have reached a length of about 4" (10cm).

Teaching the Bow to Bend . . . Making a Longbow

Form a loop (string eye) with the twisted string and adjust the dimension of the loop to the nocks.

Now, gather strands of the same color together in pairs of strands (see photo). Each color, or rather each pair of strands, should always have one long strand with one short strand.

Twist each pair of strands in itself in a clockwise direction to the right.

Teaching the Bow to Bend . . . Making a Longbow

After that, twist the pairs of strands (twisted in itself to the right) around each other to the left by putting alternately one pair of strands to the left over the other.

After three or four twists, start to taper the diameter of the string by pulling out the short ends to the side and stop twisting them with the rest of the strand.

Teaching the Bow to Bend . . . Making a Longbow

After having pulled out all the short ends, carry on twisting the long strands (twisted in itself to the right) around each other to the left until they have reached the intended string length.

The short ends sticking out at the side will then be cut off. Be careful not to damage the bow string!

Now singe off the short ends of the synthetic thread with a cigarette lighter — a small bead will form preventing the threads from slipping out.

Lastly, secure the end of the bow string with a knot and tighten it securely.

Bowyer's Knot

The bowyer's knot tightens under compression and is easy to loosen after releasing the strain. Using this knot, the bow string can easily be customized to the length of the bow.

Put the string behind the nocks of the limb.

Form a loop by putting the loose short end of the string underneath the string.

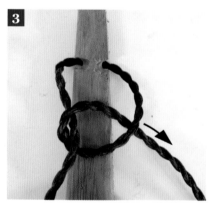

Put the short end through the loop ...

... and bring it over the string and go through the loop for the second time.

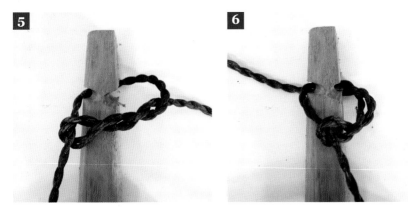

Put the short end around the back of the limb, so that both strands lie in front of the limb. Start pulling each strand successively in the same direction (towards yourself) until the knot rests tightly around the nocks.

Finally, position the knot around the nocks and tighten it again securely.

Glossary

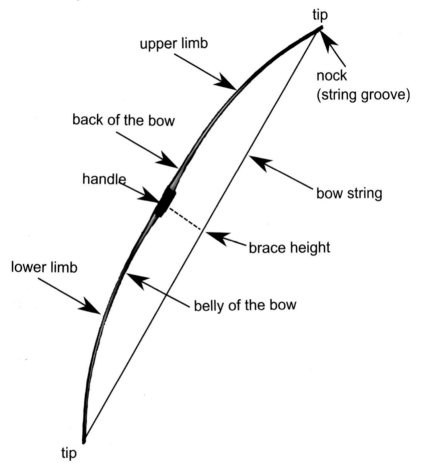

Back of the Bow: The outward side of the bow turning away from the archer, facing the target (mainly tensile strain).

Belly of the Bow: The inward side of the bow facing the archer (mainly compressive strain).

Bow Stave: Piece of wood with roughly sawn out shape of the bow.

Bow String: String going from one nock to the other that transfers the stored energy to the arrow; twisted of several strands, nowadays usually of synthetic material.

Bow Stringer: String with leather caps at each end for bracing and unbracing the bow. This is highly recommended for use during the tillering process and also with the finished bow!

Bowyer's Knot: Knot for Flemish splice bow strings, which allows for adjusting the length of the bow string.

Brace Height: The breadth of a fist with the thumb stuck out; measurement for the correct distance of the string from the bow.

Draw Length: Distance between back of the bow and bow string at full draw, measured in inches.

Draw Weight: Force that is needed to pull a bow up to full draw length, measured in pounds (lbs).

Finish: Treatment of the surface of the bow with wax or oil.

Flemish Splice String: Bow string made of several strands with a spliced loop (string eye) at one end.

Growth Ring: Annual ring conveying the amount of wood added during a single growth period.

Handle: Middle part of the bow where the bow is held.

Inch: Unit of measurement, corresponds to ca. 25.4mm (1").

lbs.: Pound, unit of measurement, corresponds to ca. 454 grams.

Limb: The bending parts of a bow — a bow has an upper limb and a lower limb.

Nock: Nock groove, string groove, grooves at the end of each limb to hold the bow string.

String Eye: Loop at the end of a bow string for stringing the bow between the nocks.

Tiller: Bending proportions of the limbs from the side view.

Tillering: Process of removing wood from a stave to get to the intended bending of the bow.

Tillering Stick: A board with notches to clamp in the bow stave during the tillering process.

Tillering String: Extra strong string for the tillering process, adjustable with bowyer's knot.

Tips: Ends of the limbs.

ABOUT THE AUTHORS

Working with wood has always been fascinating for us, so it was only a small step from bow shooting to the first self-made bow. That was about ten years ago. What followed was the study of many, many books and movies and many, many hours of tillering and experimenting until we finally got the feel for it.

About eight years ago, we made the decision to start our own business as bowyers. In the meantime, we have built quite a few bows of different types. Most of our happy customers though prefer the traditional English longbow.

Michael Wlotzka

Linda Schilling

Bow with siyahs, modeled on illustrations from the medieval Crusader's Bible (length 56-3/4" or 144cm, 30 lbs at max. 26 inches).

However, replicas modeled on historical findings like the Meare Heath bow or the Holmegaard bow have also become increasingly popular.

Many of our customers have said, "Oh, it has always been one of my childhood dreams to make my own bow," so we started to offer bow making workshops and always share the joy with our customers when they proudly go home with their first self-made bow.

The tiller tool is a helpful device to mark the "stiff" sections on the limb of the braced bow stave, allowing you to check the tiller quickly and easily with the necessary accuracy. With the brass screw, the

integrated pencil can be adjusted accurately to a tenth of an inch/ millimeter, making it possible to identify very small inconsistencies in the tiller.

The spokeshave allows an accurate removal of fine shavings, precisely and properly. It is also ideal for irregular grain direction. The one shown here is made of Wenge wood while the lock nuts, the threads, and the sole are made of brass. The plane blade is positioned at an angle of about 90° against the work piece. The cutting edge of the blade has a burr that allows the removal of very thin shavings.

Meare Heath bow with binding on the limbs.

CENTIMETERS TO INCHES BY INCREMENTS OF 1

Centimeters	Inches	Centimeters	Inches	Centimeters	Inches
0.000 cm	0 in.	101.60 cm	40 in.	203.20 cm	80 in.
2.5400 cm	1 in.	104.14 cm	41 in.	205.74 cm	81 in.
5.0800 cm	2 in.	106.68 cm	42 in.	208.28 cm	82 in.
7.6200 cm	3 in.	109.22 cm	43 in.	210.82 cm	83 in.
10.160 cm	4 in.	111.76 cm	44 in.	213.36 cm	84 in.
12.700 cm	5 in.	114.30 cm	45 in.	215.90 cm	85 in.
15.240 cm	6 in.	116.84 cm	46 in.	218.44 cm	86 in.
17.780 cm	7 in.	119.38 cm	47 in.	220.98 cm	87 in.
20.320 cm	8 in.	121.92 cm	48 in.	223.52 cm	88 in.
22.860 cm	9 in.	124.46 cm	49 in.	226.06 cm	89 in.
25.400 cm	10 in.	127.00 cm	50 in.	228.60 cm	90 in.
27.940 cm	11 in.	129.54 cm	51 in.	231.14 cm	91 in.
30.480 cm	12 in.	132.08 cm	52 in.	233.68 cm	92 in.
33.020 cm	13 in.	134.62 cm	53 in.	236.22 cm	93 in.
35.560 cm	14 in.	137.16 cm	54 in.	238.76 cm	94 in.
38.100 cm	15 in.	139.70 cm	55 in.	241.30 cm	95 in.
40.640 cm	16 in.	142.24 cm	56 in.	243.84 cm	96 in.
43.180 cm	17 in.	144.78 cm	57 in.	246.38 cm	97 in.
45.720 cm	18 in.	147.32 cm	58 in.	248.92 cm	98 in.
48.260 cm	19 in.	149.86 cm	59 in.	251.46 cm	99 in.
50.800 cm	20 in.	152.40 cm	60 in.	254.00 cm	100 in.
53.340 cm	21 in.	154.94 cm	61 in.	256.54 cm	101 in.
55.880 cm	22 in.	157.48 cm	62 in.	259.08 cm	102 in.
58.420 cm	23 in.	160.02 cm	63 in.	261.62 cm	103 in.
60.960 cm	24 in.	162.56 cm	64 in.	264.16 cm	104 in.
63.500 cm	25 in.	165.10 cm	65 in.	266.70 cm	105 in.
66.040 cm	26 in.	167.64 cm	66 in.	269.24 cm	106 in.
68.580 cm	27 in.	170.18 cm	67 in.	271.78 cm	107 in.
71.120 cm	28 in.	172.72 cm	68 in.	274.32 cm	108 in.
73.660 cm	29 in.	175.26 cm	69 in.	276.86 cm	109 in.
76.200 cm	30 in.	177.80 cm	70 in.	279.40 cm	110 in.
78.740 cm	31 in.	180.34 cm	71 in.	281.94 cm	111 in.
81.280 cm	32 in.	182.88 cm	72 in.	284.48 cm	112 in.
83.820 cm	33 in.	185.42 cm	73 in.	287.02 cm	113 in.
86.360 cm	34 in.	187.96 cm	74 in.	289.56 cm	114 in.
88.900 cm	35 in.	190.50 cm	75 in.	292.10 cm	115 in.
91.440 cm	36 in.	193.04 cm	76 in.	294.64 cm	116 in.
93.980 cm	37 in.	195.58 cm	77 in.	297.18 cm	117 in.
96.520 cm	38 in.	198.12 cm	78 in.	299.72 cm	118 in.
99.060 cm	39 in.	200.66 cm	79 in.	302.26 cm	119 in.

Centimeters	Inches	Centimeters	Inches
304.80 cm	120 in.	406.40 cm	160 in.
307.34 cm	121 in.	408.94 cm	161 in.
309.88 cm	122 in.	411.48 cm	162 in.
312.42 cm	123 in.	414.02 cm	163 in.
314.96 cm	124 in.	416.56 cm	164 in.
317.50 cm	125 in.	419.10 cm	165 in.
320.04 cm	126 in.	421.64 cm	166 in.
322.58 cm	127 in.	424.18 cm	167 in.
325.12 cm	128 in.	426.72 cm	168 in.
327.66 cm	129 in.	429.26 cm	169 in.
330.20 cm	130 in.	431.80 cm	170 in.
332.74 cm	131 in.	434.34 cm	171 in.
335.28 cm	132 in.	436.88 cm	172 in.
337.82 cm	133 in.	439.42 cm	173 in.
340.36 cm	134 in.	441.96 cm	174 in.
342.90 cm	135 in.	444.50 cm	175 in.
345.44 cm	136 in.	447.04 cm	176 in.
347.98 cm	137 in.	449.58 cm	177 in.
350.52 cm	138 in.	452.12 cm	178 in.
353.06 cm	139 in.	454.66 cm	179 in.
355.60 cm	140 in.		
358.14 cm	141 in.		
360.68 cm	142 in.		
363.22 cm	143 in.		
365.76 cm	144 in.		
368.30 cm	145 in.		
370.84 cm	146 in.		
373.38 cm	147 in.		
375.92 cm	148 in.		
378.46 cm	149 in.		
381.00 cm	150 in.		
383.54 cm	151 in.		
386.08 cm	152 in.		
388.62 cm	153 in.		
391.16 cm	154 in.		
393.70 cm	155 in.		
396.24 cm	156 in.		
398.78 cm	157 in.		
401.32 cm	158 in.		
403.86 cm	159 in.		

CENTIMETERS TO INCHES BY INCREMENTS OF 0.1

Centimeters	Inches
0.0000 cm	0.0000 in.
0.25400 cm	0.10000 in.
0.50800 cm	0.20000 in.
0.76200 cm	0.30000 in.
1.0160 cm	0.40000 in.
1.2700 cm	0.50000 in.
1.5240 cm	0.60000 in.
1.7780 cm	0.70000 in.
2.0320 cm	0.80000 in.
2.2860 cm	0.90000 in.
2.5400 cm	1.0000 in.